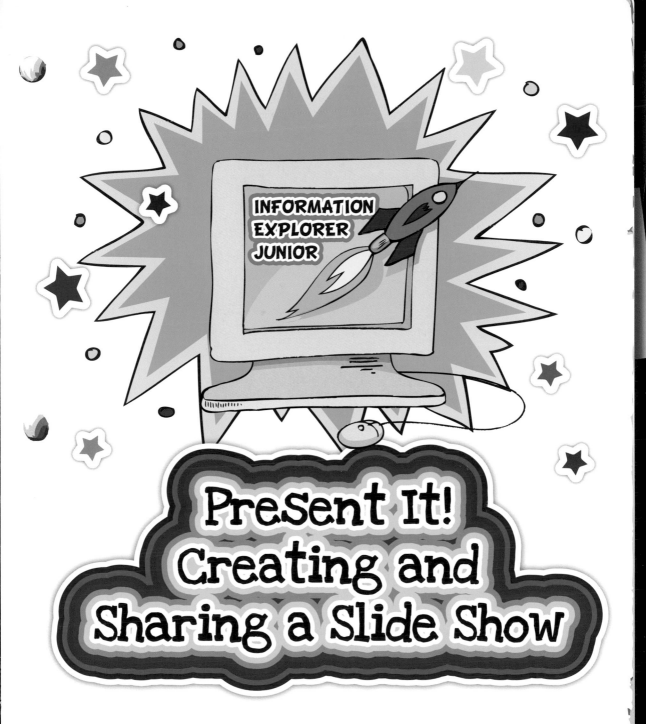

INFORMATION EXPLORER JUNIOR

Present It! Creating and Sharing a Slide Show

by Ann Truesdell

CHERRY LAKE PUBLISHING · ANN ARBOR, MICHIGAN

A NOTE TO PARENTS AND TEACHERS: Please remind your children how to stay safe online before they do the activities in this book.

CHERRY
LAKE
Publishing

A NOTE TO KIDS: Always remember your safety comes first!

Published in the United States of America
by Cherry Lake Publishing
Ann Arbor, Michigan
www.cherrylakepublishing.com

Content Adviser: Gail Dickinson, PhD, Associate
Professor, Old Dominion University, Norfolk, Virginia

Photo Credits: Cover, ©Tyler Olson/Shutterstock.com; pages 4, 6, 12, 17, 19, and
21, ©Sarah Cheriton-Jones/Shutterstock.com; page 5, ©Aditya Kok/Dreamstime.
com; page 7, ©Monkey Business Images/Shutterstock.com; page 13, ©Tatiana
Morozova/Shutterstock.com; page 14, ©Opka/Shutterstock.com; page 16 (top and
center), ©Anan Kaewkhammul/Shutterstock.com; page 16 (bottom), ©Vetapi/
Shutterstock.com.

Library of Congress Cataloging-in-Publication Data
Truesdell, Ann, author.
  Present it! creating and sharing a slideshow / by Ann Truesdell.
    pages cm. — (Information explorer junior)
  Summary: "Learn how to create informative and entertaining slideshow
presentations" — Provided by publisher.
  Audience: Grades K to 3.
  Includes bibliographical references and index.
  ISBN 978-1-63137-787-7 (lib. bdg.) — ISBN 978-1-63137-807-2 (pbk.) —
ISBN 978-1-63137-847-8 (e-book) — ISBN 978-1-63137-827-0 (pdf)
  1. Presentation graphics software—Juvenile literature. 2. Multimedia systems—
Juvenile literature. I. Title. II. Series: Information explorer junior.
  P93.52.T78 2014
  006.6—dc23   2014001365

Cherry Lake Publishing would like to acknowledge the work of The Partnership for
21st Century Skills. Please visit www.p21.org for more information.

Printed in the United States of America
Corporate Graphics Inc.
July 2014

Table of Contents

CHAPTER ONE

Share with a Slide Show

Eddy's teacher has asked him to create a presentation about tigers for the class. He is excited! He will speak in front of everyone. He will also have a slide show to share! A slide show displays a series of screens called slides. Slides use pictures, words, videos, music, or graphs as **visual aids**. They

Slides can help an audience understand a presentation.

4

Slide shows are used in many different settings.

help the audience understand what the presenter is talking about.

People in business use slide shows to share their ideas. Teachers use them to teach students new information. Students can use slide shows to show what they have learned. You can make a slide show on almost any computer. When it is time to give a presentation, you can connect the computer to a projector or a video screen. Then everyone can see your slides!

To get a copy of this activity, visit
www.cherrylakepublishing.com/activities.

Try This

There are many computer programs you can use to create a slide show. Microsoft PowerPoint and Apple Keynote are two of the most widely used slide show programs. There are also Web sites that let you create presentations online. These sites include Prezi, SlideShare, Zoho Show, Empressr, and Prezentit. Finally, there are many slide show apps that you can use on tablet computers. Ask an adult to help you access a slide show program on a computer or other device. Try it out! What can you create for fun?

CHAPTER TWO

Just the Facts

A presenter should collect a lot of interesting, useful information.

Eddy reads about his topic in books. He also looks for information on the Internet. Then he organizes all of his facts into a slide show.

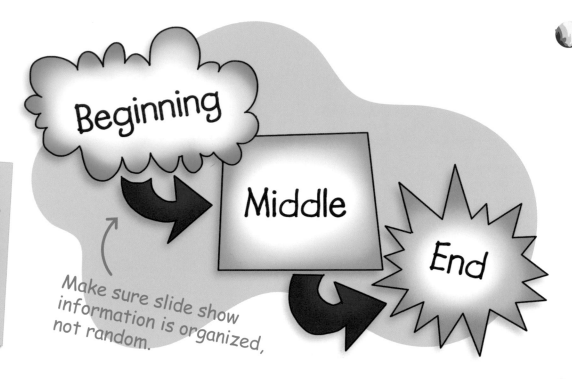

Make sure slide show information is organized, not random.

Presentations have a beginning, middle, and end. This makes it easier for the audience to follow what the presenter is talking about. Eddy starts with the basics. He discusses what tigers look like and where they live. Eddy adds more specific details in the middle of his presentation. He describes how tigers live. He also poses a problem: tigers may die out soon. At the end of his slide show, Eddy wraps things up. He explains what the audience can do to save tigers.

At first, Eddy plans to include a whole paragraph on a slide. But his sister says it looks boring. There's too much text for his audience to read. Eddy's dad suggests breaking the text into short bullet points instead. Bullet points are small dots that show different ideas in a list. Each bullet point is followed by a few words or a short sentence.

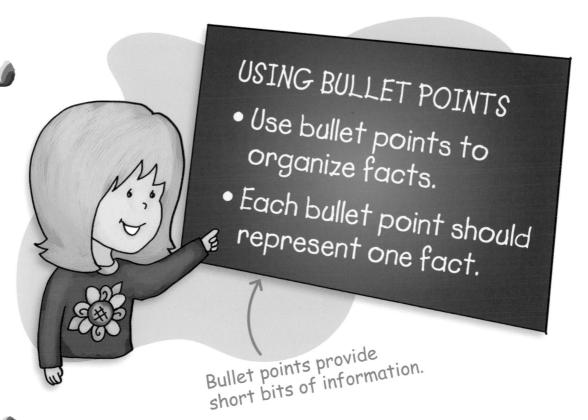

USING BULLET POINTS
- Use bullet points to organize facts.
- Each bullet point should represent one fact.

Bullet points provide short bits of information.

Try This

The order of your slides is very important. If you present information out of order, your audience might be confused.

Imagine you are helping Eddy prepare his presentation. You have created four slides with facts. The title of each slide is listed below. Which order would you put them in? Why?

A. "What Tigers Eat"
B. "What Is a Tiger?"
C. "Tigers Are Endangered: How Can You Help?"
D. "Tiger Cubs"

Answers: You might order your slides like this: B, A, D, C. Another possible order might be B, D, A, C.

Slide B comes first because it gives background information to your audience about what a tiger is. Slides D and A come next. They help you tell your story by giving further information about tigers. You end with slide C because it will leave your audience thinking about what they can do to help tigers.

Make sure the order of your slides makes sense.

CHAPTER THREE

Show Off Your Stripes

Photos can make your presentation more interesting
and informative.

Slide show presentations need more than just
words. Putting pictures on a presentation's
slides will keep an audience interested.
Pictures can also make a presentation easier

You can use photos to help explain different parts of your topic.

to understand. Images should add important information to a presentation. For example, Eddy's presentation includes a slide about tiger cubs. He adds a photo of a tiger cub to that slide to show his audience what a cub looks like.

Not all images are helpful. Many presentation programs come with built-in clip art. Clip art is usually made up of cartoonish drawings. A clip art picture of a

A map is a good image to use to show where tigers live.

tiger is not as useful as a photograph of a real tiger! It doesn't give the audience any useful information about tigers.

Animated clip art, such as a cartoon tiger running, is not helpful either. However, Eddy does want to show a tiger in action. He decides to **embed** a video of a running tiger in his presentation. Short videos can make a presentation very interesting! In some cases, such as showing how a tiger moves, a video clip would be a better choice than a picture.

Graphs, charts, timelines, and maps can also be added to a presentation. Eddy gives credit to where he found each picture, video, or other visual aid.

A great place to go for free pictures and videos is http://search .creativecommons.org.

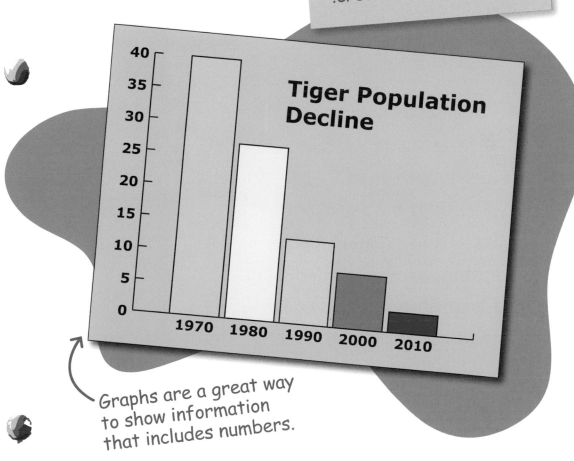

Graphs are a great way to show information that includes numbers.

Try This

Let's add images to Eddy's slide show. Look at the slide titles and images below. Which pictures belong on which slides?

A

Slides

1. "What Tigers Eat"
2. "What Is a Tiger?"
3. "Tigers Are Endangered: How Can You Help?"
4. "Tiger Cubs"

B

C

Images

A. Picture of a tiger cub
B. Picture of an adult tiger
C. Picture of a deer or wild pig
D. Graph showing the decline in the tiger population

D

Answers: 1-C, 2-B, 3-D, 4-A

CHAPTER FOUR

Make It Shine

All the fonts and photos on a slide should go well together.

It is finally time for Eddy to design his presentation. This means choosing **fonts** and colors. He also needs to decide how to organize the different slides. The design should make it easy to see the words and images on the slides.

Eddy wants to choose fonts that are easy to read. First, he tries a cursive font. But when he shows the slides to his mom, she has trouble reading the text. Fancy fonts look pretty, but are harder to read. Very basic fonts are clearer. Eddy's dad suggests he use Verdana, Arial, or Times New Roman.

Eddy also needs the text to be big enough for everyone to see, no matter where they sit. Font sizes from 18 to 24 points are usually good for presentations.

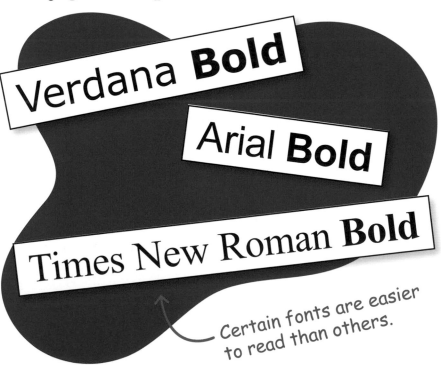

Verdana **Bold**

Arial **Bold**

Times New Roman **Bold**

Certain fonts are easier to read than others.

Some backgrounds can be distracting.

Eddy tries different backgrounds for his slides. He finds that solid-colored backgrounds that are not too bright work best. Very bright colors make it hard to read the words on the slides. Text should stick out against the background color. This is called **contrast**. A light-colored background and dark text is a great contrast. A dark background with light text also works. Eddy chooses a dark green background and pale yellow text.

Tiger Cubs
- Cubs have a gestation period of 103 days.
- After tigers are born they stay with their mother for 2 years.
- When tigers are born, they weigh about 2 pounds.
- Tigers live 10 to 15 years.
- The Caspian, Javan, and Bali tigers are all extinct.

Too much text will leave no room for pictures.

Next, Eddy designs each slide's layout. He tries different ways of organizing text and images. The computer program he uses came with some **templates** to help him. He finds that three to five bullet points per slide works best. He only includes one or two pictures on each slide. He tried fitting more, but it looked too crowded.

Finally, Eddy adds a title to each slide to tell what the slide is about. The title font is bigger than the font used for the bullet points. He shows the finished presentation to his family. They love it!

To get a copy of this activity, visit www.cherrylakepublishing.com/activities.

Try This

Which slide is the best for sharing information about tiger cubs? Why?

Did Slide C grab your attention first? The strong contrast, useful photo, and easy-to-read facts make it the best slide. Now it's your turn! What would you share in your slide show?

Tiger Cubs
- Cubs have a gestation period of 103 days.
- After tigers are born they stay with their mother for 2 years.
- When tigers are born, they weigh about 2 pounds.
- Tigers live 10 to 15 years.
- The Caspian, Javan, and Bali tigers are all extinct.

 A

Tiger Cubs
- An average litter is 2 or 3 cubs.
- Cubs weigh 2 pounds at birth.
- Tiger cubs leave their mothers when they are 2 years old.

B

Tiger Cubs
- An average litter is 2 or 3 cubs.
- Cubs weigh 2 pounds at birth.
- Tiger cubs leave their mothers when they are 2 years old.

C

Glossary

contrast (KAHN-trast) the difference between two things

embed (em-BED) to make something a part of something else, such as placing a video file into a slide show presentation

fonts (FAHNTS) styles of text

templates (TEM-plits) documents or patterns that are used to create similar documents

visual aids (VIZH-oo-uhl AYDZ) things people can look at to help them understand ideas and facts in a presentation

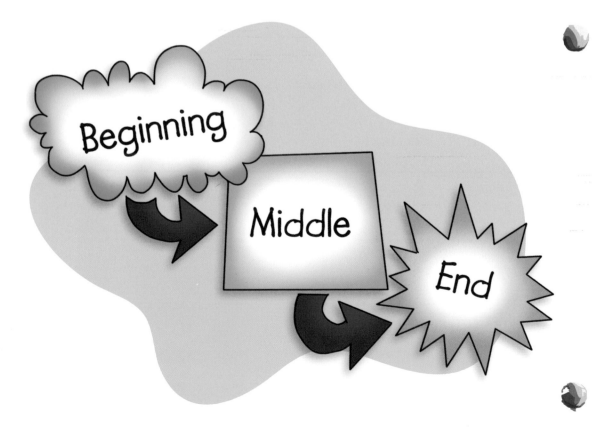

Find Out More

BOOKS

Fontichiaro, Kristin. *Find Out Firsthand: Using Primary Sources.* Ann Arbor, MI: Cherry Lake Publishing, 2013.

StJohn, Amanda. *How to Find Information Online.* Mankato, MN: Childs World, 2013.

WEB SITES

Creative Commons—CC Search

http://search.creativecommons.org

Creative Commons' CC Search looks for images, videos, and other media files on the Internet. You can use these materials for free in your presentation.

KidsSpace: Research Skills

http://kidsspace.torontopubliclibrary.ca/research.html

This site offers pointers and resources you can use when you do research for your presentation online.

Index

About the Author

Ann Truesdell is a school library media specialist and teacher in Michigan. She and her husband, Mike, are the proud parents of James, Charlotte, and Matilda. Ann enjoys traveling and reading.